I0007786

THE
SOCIAL
MEDIA
Makeover

2nd Edition

Tisha Holman

Copyright © 2018 Tisha Holman
All rights reserved.
ISBN: 9781730877964

DEDICATION

This book is dedicated to all of the brands, entrepreneurs and organizations seeking the knowledge to improve how they approach social media and the team of social media professionals they lead.

Why the Social Media Makeover?

Social media defined: *Digital platforms typically comprised of websites or applications that facilitate social networking, information sharing, research and communication.*

If your business or organization is not playing competitively in the social media arena, then you are leaving money on the table. What changes do you need to implement concerning your brand's social media strategy to see a return on your time investment? Social media affords you access to a multitude of clients the average small business owner or organization would not usually be able to tap into. It is estimated there are approximately 2.3 billion active users on social media. That is a huge market share of people that are just waiting for you to introduce your brand to them!

According to a recent study conducted by the Pew Research Center, sixty-nine percent of the public uses some type of social media. In a Forbes Magazine article, Facebook COO Sheryl Sandberg stated that there are over sixty million businesses globally with active Facebook pages, with the majority being small and medium-sized businesses. She also goes on to say many small businesses struggle to manage their online presence.

Do you fall into this category?

Maintaining a formidable presence on social media gives you a competitive advantage that will increase your Search Engine Optimization (SEO) ranking, customer loyalty, brand recognition and ultimately your bottom line. What are you doing to ensure your brand stands out in the digital and social media spaces? This book is written based on strategies, tactics and principles that have been proven successful for the small business owner and major corporation alike. There are aspects of this that may seem a bit daunting at first, but it is all designed to give your social media platforms the makeover needed to change the trajectory of your business, and move it toward success.

Table of Contents

You Have To Talk the Talk

The world of social media has its own jargon that can be very confusing and even intimidating to those who are novices in this realm. I have placed this glossary of terms at the front of the book, so that as you encounter terms that may not be familiar, you can easily come here to get clarity. The Social Media Makeover is meant to make the concept of social media simpler for you. I hope you find these pages to be useful as you navigate your journey towards a better social media strategy.

As one who manages a team of social media professionals, you will need to speak "social media" fluently. This terminology will be important as you broaden your understanding and knowledge of this very important area of your digital footprint. You may also consider integrating some of these terms into your standard operating procedures or training documents. Your subordinates will know this lingo like the back of their hand and expect that you will too.

Algorithm
The science social media networks use to filter, rank and prioritize the posts that show up on user feeds and timelines.

Amplification Rate
The number of times a particular post was shared on the social media platform.

Analytics
The collection of data from social media activity most often used to gauge the success or failure of social media strategies and tactics.

Assets
Videos, static images or any other content to be used as a part of a brand's marketing mix.

Automation
The utilization of social media scheduling tools to publish content and engage with your followers.

Avatar
An icon or image used to represent a person.

Brand Ambassadors/Evangelists:
The end-users your brand/organization has that help increase awareness of your brand on social media as demonstrated by their engagement and advocacy across platforms.

Brand Awareness
The extent to which potential customers are familiar with the differentiating qualities and images of a brand.

Brand Harmonization
The concept that all elements within the esthetic of a brand have consistency.

Call to Action
An instruction to an audience meant to elicit some type of response.

Click-Throughs
The number of clicks on a link to a post on a given social network

Content Marketing
A strategic plan based on connecting with your target audience via the curation of valuable, engaging content.

Conversion Rate
The percentage of users who take the desired action or respond to a Call To Action.

Crisis Management
The process an organization has in place to mitigate the impact of risk of varying scope on social media – (PR issues, social and political issues, security breaches)

Engagement
The measurement of various interactions with content that has been posted on social media.

Evergreen Content
Content that is timeless and will always be pertinent and of interest to your follower base.

Filter
Effects that can be applied to enhance images and video content.

Followers
The people following your social media channels

Fraudulent Accounts
Social media accounts created with the nefarious intent to impersonate another person or entity.

Geotargeting
A feature that allows content to be shared specifically with geographically defined areas.

Graphics Interchange Format (GIF)
A popular file type used to create more engaging video and static content.

Hashtags
Content aggregators used to increase the reach of social media posts, and make them more searchable.

Influencer
A person or entity with a large, highly engaged follower base on social media most often leveraged by others to engender Brand Awareness or products, services or causes.

Impressions
The number of times a particular piece of content is shown in an end-users feed, regardless of engagement.

Listening

The assessment of the general consensus of what end-users are saying about brands/organizations across social media platforms.

Organic Content

Social media posts without any paid campaign attached.

Paid Social Media Content

Social media posts with a paid campaign attached with the intent to increase the reach and engagement of the content.

Post Reach

The number of people who see a particular piece of content in their feed or timeline at least once.

Referral Rate

The measure of traffic directed to a website from an outside source.

Search Engine Optimization (SEO)

Methods used to increase traffic to a website by improving its search engine page rank.

Sentiment

The overall "mood" or impression of a particular piece of content typically described as positive, negative or neutral. This is usually determined by an algorithmic assessment of language used on the post.

(Social media) Strategy

A targeted plan or method for achieving a particular goal.

(Social media) Tactic
The actual means used to achieve a goal or objective.

Target Audience
A specifically determined demographic of end-users thought to be ideal consumers of a product or service, or have a unique interest in a cause or organization.

Trending (Topic)
When a story, topic or hashtag has a high simultaneous engagement with end-users. Topics can trend regionally, nationally or globally.

Troll
Someone who purposely joins conversations with the intent to cause dissension, usually with disparaging and offensive remarks.

Urchin Tracking Module (UTM) Code
A tracking marker added to a URL used to identify referral sources, mediums or special campaigns.

Verified Account
An account, usually an influencer, celebrity, brand or public figure determined to be authentic by a vetting process conducted by the social media platform administrators to mitigate fraudulent activity.

It's Time for an Audit!

"Progress is impossible without change, and those who cannot change their minds cannot change anything."

– George Bernard Shaw

Before you begin the Social Media Makeover, you have to do an audit. This audit is nothing like the kind the IRS performs, but is nevertheless designed to take an assessment of your social media accounts to determine where your areas of opportunity exist. Once the data is collected, it will be the foundation for your new social media strategy.

You have to take an honest look at the type of content you are posting, how it is performing and whether or not it is yielding the desired results. It may be challenging to look at this with a critical eye, but it is important to flag the things that really are not working for you. Additionally, you may find it helpful to take a look at what your "competitors" are doing to see any differences in user engagement, and tactics they are using that may be more effective for your target audience. I used quotation marks around the word competitor because I have always felt that word is relative. It is wise to have a healthy awareness of what others in your industry are doing, but do not allow yourself to become consumed with their efforts to the point you begin to emulate what they are doing. The consequence of this is you can inadvertently become discouraged because they appear to be seeing greater success than you may be experiencing.

Each social media platform has its own rules of engagement. For Search Engine Optimization (SEO) purposes, it is a good idea to maintain a presence on all of the major channels. Do a periodic check for new social networks that may align with your business or industry so you stay ahead of trends in the digital marketing space.

I've created this checklist, albeit not necessarily exhaustive for every industry vertical, to assist you with your audit. You may find it helpful to create a spreadsheet to easily track, review and share this information.

Social Media Audit Checklist

- ✓ Who has access to your social media accounts?
- ✓ Where are log-in credentials stored?
- ✓ How are you managing the publishing of social media content?
- ✓ Do any copycat or fraudulent accounts exist that falsely represent your brand?
- ✓ Does Brand Harmonization exist with your social media handles?
- ✓ Profile Images – Do you have properly sized avatars, profile photos, icons, cover photos, etc.?
- ✓ Profile Data – Is the copy in your bio, company descriptions, Website URL's, phone numbers and email addresses current?
- ✓ What is your current posting frequency for all content types (text, links, static images, video, etc.)?
- ✓ What is your current number of followers?
- ✓ What are your engagement rates?
- ✓ What is your highest and lowest performing content?
- ✓ Where are your highest referral rates to your website coming from?
- ✓ Is your current content strategy in alignment with your Buyer Persona?
- ✓ Are your social media accounts cross-promoted on your other digital channels?
- ✓ Perform a Competitive Audit on your industry peers to identify areas that seem to be highly effective. What are your observations about their content strategy?

- ✓ Is your Unique Selling and Value Proposition clear in your content strategy?
- ✓ What tools, apps, and resources are being used to create and post content?
- ✓ What is the Return On Investment for any Ad Spends you have in place?
- ✓ How are images and videos sourced and created?

The 'Harvard Business Review' sums up the importance of the social media audit perfectly. "The social media audit tool helps marketers make sense of the many opportunities these platforms offer by allowing them to see their brands from the perspective of the customer."

A modification of the initial social media audit you perform will become a regular part of managing your social media platforms after you complete the Social Media Makeover. You will need to take a frequent, periodic assessment of how content is performing on your social media accounts. Each social media platform has its own set of metrics that can be measured to determine whether or not content you are posting is performing well. You will have to determine what metrics are most important to measure success for your organization. You will need to run these reports so you can make adjustments to content if it is not resonating with your intended target audience. Each of the social media platforms have native tools that can help you take a deeper dive into the analytics of your content. There are also some great tools available that can pull analytics reports from all of your social media platforms and house the data in one place.

Mind Your Business!

Who will be the person in your organization delegated to conduct the social media audit?

_____

_____

_____

_____

Who are the influencers within your industry vertical?

_____

_____

_____

_____

Who are your "competitors"?

_____

_____

_____

_____

Discover your "Why": Laying the Groundwork

"Productivity is never an accident. It is always the result of a commitment to excellence, intelligent planning and focused effort."

– Paul J. Meyer

The strategy for your social media should not be haphazard and merely a random output of details shared about your business or organization. In order for you to see success and a return on your time investment, there must be a method to your madness. The beginning of building a masterful social media strategy is discovering your "why". To be truly effective in the digital marketing and social media spaces, your efforts have to be diligent, targeted and specific.

Diligent – Targeted – Specific

Who is Your Target Audience?

It is critical that you figure out who you are talking to on social media. Knowing who your target audience/client is will help you to curate content that is of interest to them. If you are not sharing content or ideas that piques the interest of who you are trying to reach, you are not going to see the conversions you are looking for (sales, traffic to website, increased engagement, etc.). You must develop personas for your organization.

Personas are almost like a dossier of sorts, as they are intended to paint a clear picture of your target audience. Developing personas for your core and target audiences is an essential part of your strategic approach to digital marketing, social media in particular. Your core audience is the constituency of people that are already within your brand's ecosystem. Your target audience is the constituency of people you want to attract into your brand's ecosystem.

Knowing your audience well helps you develop well-executed and informed content that is tailored to the people you want to reach most. If you do not have a strong grasp of the needs, interests, characteristics and personality of your audience, you cannot connect with them in an impactful and meaningful way. Laying the groundwork for meaningful connections with your audience is the ultimate goal here.

Consider the attributes below as you develop the persona for your audiences:

- Background
- Age
- Gender
- Income
- Education
- Occupation
- Family Structure
  - Who are the decision makers?
- Geographic Location
- Religious background
- Platform preferences
  - Where do they hang out online? How frequently do they engage online?
- Keywords
  - What are they searching for online? (This will help you develop effective paid media campaigns)
- Challenges
  - What problem can you solve for them?

When your personas are completed, others should be able to look at them and have a strong understanding of the target and core audiences for your brand or organization. Depending on your findings, you may discover that there are several personas for your brand, and that is okay, expected even. You will be able to fill in some of the blanks for this task from an established familiarity with your audience. However, in order for this to be most effective, you should be using data that you have gathered from your constituents and market research to draw intelligent conclusions.

Your decisions should always be data-driven

An integral facet to discovering your "why" is clearly defining what your goals are for your presence on social media. Paul J. Meyer describes the elements of S.M.A.R.T. goals in his book, "Attitude is Everything: If You Want to Succeed Above and Beyond".

Let's delve a bit deeper in to what S.M.A.R.T. goals are and how you can implement this formula to get started in the discovery of your why!

Specific
Measurable
Achievable
Realistic
Time Bound

Specific

One has a greater likelihood of accomplishing goals that are targeted and specific. Identify the Who, What, When, Where, Why and How for your goals. Do your best to be as detailed as possible in this section, as it will set the tone for the rest of the process. Goals that are too general will bottleneck later in the S.M.A.R.T. formula. Keep your goals both simple and clear.

Measurable

How are you going to measure the tangible results of the goals you have set? That can vary greatly depending on what your objectives are for having a presence on social media. Defining checkpoints for your goals not only keeps you motivated along your journey, but it also allows you to make any adjustments that may be required to keep you on track.

Achievable

Are the goals you have set attainable within the pool of resources you have available to you? You have to be sure that you can make this goal happen with the people, tools and systems you have in place. Additionally, do not set goals that are too low – set goals that are going to stretch and develop you both personally and professionally.

Realistic

Goals can be realistic and lofty. In the world of social media, it wouldn't be prudent to task yourself with gaining one million followers on a social network in a week's time. However, you can still challenge yourself with gaining more followers, but with a more realistic and gradual rubric. The objective is to accomplish the goals, and set yourself up for success. Ultimately, what truly makes a goal "realistic" is your sincere belief that you can accomplish it! Belief in yourself is a powerful tool to have in your arsenal!

Time Bound

If you do not define the timeframe in which it will take you to accomplish your goals, they inadvertently become this open-ended idea you have that likely will not come to fruition. Set realistic deadlines, and hold yourself accountable to meeting them.

Mind Your Business!

What is your brand or organization's "why" for having a presence on social media?

_____

_____

_____

_____

What do you know about your core and target audiences?

_____

_____

_____

_____

List four S.M.A.R.T. goals you can set for your social media:

_____

_____

_____

_____

_____

_____

_____

_____

A Brand in Demand

"Brands must become architects of community."

– Simon Mainwaring

The American Marketing Association defines a brand as "A name, term, design, symbol or any other feature that identifies one seller's good or service as distinct from those of other sellers." What differentiates your business or organization from other's in your industry? Have you laid a foundation for a sustainable brand that can withstand changes in trends and client needs? It is important that people who engage with you on your social media channels see Brand Harmony across all platforms. Social media handles, choice and quality of imagery, your logo, language and content are all extensions of your brand. Having consistency in these areas gives you credibility, and will increase customer loyalty. A solid brand creates trust, which in turn creates clients who become ambassadors for your company.

Authenticity Matters

Beyond your brand being consistent with the collateral displayed on your digital spaces, you have to be cognizant of the messaging that is used on your social media accounts. Have you established the voice of your brand? The voice of your brand needs to have a relatable element, you cannot be all business all of the time. People have to feel like more than what you are offering, there is something about you that also resonates with them. Strike a healthy balance between what your true objectives are on social media, and giving people the occasional calculated glimpse into the person behind the scenes. Although your posts should always include some type of call-to-action, knowing who your target audience is helps you finesse the art of building relationship, which subsequently makes you a part of their daily routine. According to the 2017 Consumer Content Report conducted by Stakla, eighty-six percent of those surveyed say that authenticity is important when deciding what brands they will like and support. These findings reiterate the value of developing thorough personas, and they shape communication with your audience. The Stakla report also asserts that, on average, twenty percent of consumers, and thirty percent of millennials unfollowed a brand on social media because they felt their content was inauthentic. Don't allow your brand to become a casualty of the results of an inauthentic social media presence. In today's competitive digital marketplace, authenticity and transparency are a significant factor in your brand's unique value proposition.

It's Emotional

Great brands resonate with their constituents by evoking emotion. In this instance, emotion does not necessarily mean in the touchy-feely sense. More so, your brand has to show passion to its audience. Passion can come through: the empirical example of clear vision, excellence in service or product delivery, strong leadership, or through simple inspiration. Whatever the conduit of delivery is for your particular brand, it has to be compelling, and it has to pull your audience in…and keep them there.

Style Guide

A style guide is the way in which an organization establishes a baseline for not only communication and tactics (visual and written) within cross-functional teams, but also those outside of your organization about various attributes of your brand identity. Here are elements that should be included in your brand's style guide:

- **Mission/Vision Statement** - Verbiage from this could be used to guide the copy curated and used for:
  - Blog content
  - Ad copy
  - Visual media

- **Persona** - The personas you developed should also have a visual element as they are essentially dossiers of fictional characters that describe the brand core and target audiences.
- **Color Palette** – Your brand's color palette should be clearly defined so that it is consistently used in everything produced for internal and external use.
    - The color should be coded in Pantone, Hex and RBG - When you pick them, commit to them. This will help to build brand equity with your audience.
- **Typography** - Outline the various fonts used in the copy for your brand. This is another area that needs to be committed to once it is chosen to build brand equity.
- **Approved images** - As your online presence is built, images will need to be selected for the website, and assets created for use across your digital footprint.
    - Logos - Identify "Do's and Don'ts" use cases for the brand logo
    - Pictures of leadership/key stakeholders - Obtain approved images so that key leaders are always represented in a manner with which they are comfortable.
- **Editorial Style Guide** - This should include brand taglines, slogans, and verbiage for products, events, etc. This is important to ensure messaging is consistent across all online channels.
    - This should also note what's excluded. What is the verbiage that should be never used on your brand platforms for internal and external communication?
    - This is directly connected to the brand personas - The writing style should appeal to the core persona and draw the target in.

Five ways to build a brand in demand

1. Be a problem solver!

Any seasoned entrepreneur or C-level executive will tell you that great businesses solve problems for their customers. If you want to create a brand that withstands the test of time, don't just start a business, create a product, or offer exemplary service that is the clear answer to someone's problem. Will you be the next Amazon or Google?

2. Be transparent!

Great brands are deeply authentic and transparent in every touchpoint with their constituents. Customers need to trust the brand, not just the product or service you offer. How do you respond to PR conundrums? Are you socially responsible? Is your executive leadership visible and relatable?

3. Be adaptable!

The only constant is change. Particularly in the digital space, your brand has to move and groove with new trends and technologies. Your assessment of the problem you solve for customers must be dynamic and continuous. The way you solve their problem today may not be the same way you solve it five years from now. Adapt!

4. Be great!

The world of entrepreneurship is very competitive! It is not enough for you to be simply good at what you do, you must be great. Your product or service has to be the best option for your customer. Figure out your value proposition, leverage it, and be great.

5. Be intentional!

Everything connected with your brand has to have a distinct purpose behind it. Time is our most valuable commodity – once it is gone, we cannot recoup it. With that being said, do not spend time engaging in activity, investing in resources or hanging on to people that do not help move your business forward. There should be measurable purpose in all that you do.

Mind Your Business!

Stop and consider what you want people to feel when they encounter your brand? To guide your thoughts in this exercise, what comes to mind when you think of: McDonald's, Target, Starbucks, or Walmart?

_____

_____

_____

_____

_____

_____

_____

_____

How would you describe your brand to someone?

_____

_____

_____

_____

What problem does your brand solve for your customers?

_____

_____

_____

_____

It's Handled!:
Crisis Management

"It's Handled."
        -Olivia Pope

C reating a digital footprint for your brand will inevitably be met with possible public relations conundrums. Life happens. As long as you work with and serve people, you are at a potential risk for conflict. Unfortunately, the digital space facilitates the possibly for virality which can be highly damaging to the reputation of the brand, products and its leadership. Are you prepared to handle this?

Communication Plan

No response, is the worst possible response.

You are going to need to mobilize a communication plan and you must control the narrative! Who can tell your story better you can? Start by acknowledging what happened – DO NOT allow the situation to fester. Create a flow chart that involves different stakeholders depending on the nature of the issue. Minor occurrences may not require the involvement of senior level leadership, but issues that have greater repercussions may require their input.

You may need to quickly develop graphics or even a video message that supports your explanation of the company position on the situation, or your apology. Do not engage with what I have affectionately named "thumb thugs" (people who are emboldened behind keyboards and will type reckless and disparaging comments on online platforms). Social media can be a very unyielding crowd in the midst of transgression and melee. Respond quickly, and with transparency.

According to J.D. Power, sixty-seven percent of consumers have engaged a brand's social media for customer service needs. Forty-two percent of consumers expect a response on social media within sixty minutes. This tells us that the expectation for a resolve to issues is high, and the window is small to get it handled.

Listen Up!

Conduct a keyword search to identify what the negative buzz words are, and to gather the general sentiment about what has taken place. Once you have that information, you can put some paid media tactics in place to neutralize the virality of the negative keywords.

Here a few things you may need to put into place if you find yourself having to triage a public relations disaster:

- ✓ Define the "Crisis"
- ✓ Establish your company's guideline for assessing the nature and severity of the issue at hand
- ✓ Pause/Suspend scheduled social media content until you get a grasp on the crisis
- ✓ Define what the roles and responsibilities are for all involved teams
- ✓ Develop a communication plan for external and internal updates
- ✓ Identify who the critical stakeholders are, and be sure their contact information is current and accessible
- ✓ Determine what the approval process will be for the publication of copy and messaging online
- ✓ Plan a post-crisis deconstruction of what occurred so opportunities to strengthen your crisis plan can be identified

Mind Your Business!

Who will you task to develop your organization's communication plan?

_____

_____

_____

_____

Who are the key stakeholders that need to be involved if an issue arises on social media?

_____

_____

_____

_____

How has your organization handled prior issues on social media?

_____

_____

_____

_____

Content is King

"Creativity is just connecting things. When you ask creative people how they did something, they feel a little guilty because they didn't really do it, they just saw something. It seemed obvious to them after a while. That's because they were able to connect experiences they've had and synthesize new things."

– Steve Jobs

C ontent is king and consistency is key! In the social media audit, you examined the performance of the various types of content across your social media platforms. When you completed your persona, you developed a greater sense of who your target audience is. Now with those tools in the arsenal of your social media strategy, you can begin curating amazing content that is going to make you a social media rock star! So what kinds of content can you post to enhance your social media presence?

Campaigns

What is a social media campaign? It is an initiative on social media platforms designed to increase awareness of your brand, user engagement, or sales conversions.

There has to be a method to your madness on social media. Your team needs to keep operational content in play in addition to developing campaigns that are connected special offers, events or causes. Allow me to further explain what I mean by operational content. I define operational content as standard posts that are published on your accounts on a regular, typically daily basis. An example of this might be a morning inspirational quote, a daily devotional post, or a daily live video – something that your followers know they can expect from your brand consistently. Operational content is great for "relationship building" on social media, as it helps to position you as a thought leader and expert in the space. To really see lift on your social media accounts, your team should create campaigns that are engaging, informative and visually appealing. What is the unique selling proposition for your organization? Whatever it is, develop campaigns that feed your audience and intrigue them to learn more about your brand and what your offer.

Digital Storytelling

Social media affords you the unique opportunity to tell stories about your brand that are both compelling and exciting. Trends and innovations in video and motion graphics make it possible for your graphic designers and visual storytellers to develop content that engages your followers, and impacts them in a profound way. If you want to create posts about the awesome work your brand is doing to change the world, why limit yourself by creating a still graphic that contains a picture with text, when you can produce a sixty second video clip that *shows* them what you are doing? Do you see the difference in the picture that is painted? Tell a story. Captivate your audience! Create a narrative that lets people see your brand is the answer to their most pressing questions, or the solution to the biggest problem they are facing.

If you are not using your social media to tell a compelling digital story about your brand and the way it serves people then you are not pacing to maintain a competitive edge in this space. Effective Content Marketing is also a part of your path to success on social media. Every brand or organization is selling something. Be careful to avoid excessive aggressive calls to action that have a direct sell with a financial ask. This definitely has its place, there are times when you have to come out and say, "Buy the book!" or "Register for my event!", but be strategic about it. Your brand has to speak carefully in what has become a very noisy space. Highly sales-driven campaign are increasingly becoming a weak tactic for social media – finesse the conversation through the art of "show and tell".

Leveraging the tactic of developing campaigns on social media will help keep your team structured and organized as they work to create and execute your brand's strategy.

The rules of engagement are different on all of the different social media platforms. No matter the platform, you have to give your audience relevant and engaging content, and you have got to be consistent. You are not operating at your highest level of efficacy if your strategy does not include, at a minimum, daily published content.

Let's take a closer look at the various of types of content you can use for your social media strategy:

Static and Motion Graphics
Memes, branded video content, GIF's

Web Links
Links to websites, blogs, podcasts, news

Inspiration
Quotes and positive affirmations

Promotion
Special offers and giveaways, events and conferences, product sales

Personal
A personal and relatable glimpse in to the life of the one who is behind the brand

Information
Statistics, announcements, job postings

You want to offer your audience a variety of engaging social media content that keeps them coming back for more. Keep your content fresh, relevant and HIGH QUALITY. What do I mean by high quality?

- Be diligent about the utilization of sound grammar (unless your brand identity includes some type of slang or colloquialisms).
- Always use high resolution photo and video content.
- Always be sure any links you post are live, meaning they connect to active content.
- Be sure everything you post is the best representation of your brand. Be great!

Do not be afraid to repurpose content across social media platforms. Think about how the content you create can be used as evergreen content that appears multiple way in various places.

Check out this sample list of various ways you could repurpose a video you created and posted on YouTube:

⇒ Curate a blog post based on the content in your video

⇒ Take short, quotable excepts from your video and design static assets for use on social media channels like Facebook, Instagram and Twitter

⇒ Create short, impactful video clips from the longer video on YouTube and use them on other social media channels like Facebook, Instagram and Twitter

⇒ Share links to the both the YouTube video and the blog content on Facebook, Instagram, and Twitter

These are just a few examples, but you get the gist of it. One piece of content can serve several purposes and easily help you fill vacancies on your social media content calendar.

Ideal posting frequency by social media platform

As you embark upon your Social Media Makeover, you will likely be searching for new and innovative content to really bring something fresh and exciting to your social media presence. Depending on what your social media habits were prior to beginning this journey, you may not be accustomed to posting even on a daily basis, but you have got to stretch yourself to get to that frequency.

Not posting on social media consistently is akin to having a storefront operation that is open for business with the "closed" sign in the window. Consistency in your posts lets potential clients know you are an active brand, ready to serve them.

Suggested posting frequency

Facebook
3 – 4 times per day, unless broadcasting live – A mix of all content types

Instagram
3 – 5 times per day – A combination of static images, video and motion graphics

Twitter
4 – 6 times per day – A mix of text, links, static images, video and motion graphics

YouTube
1 – 3 times per week - High quality, branded video

After I post, now what?

Once you publish content on your social media channels you need to monitor, respond to, and engage with your audience. It is a good rule of thumb to monitor your accounts for end-user feedback after each post. As you become more active in the social media environment, you will soon find out many existing and potential clients will use your social media platforms to either voice concerns or sing your praises. In either scenario, you want to be there ready to respond to them in a timely manner, because doing so will develop ambassadors for your brand. We already know that great brands solve problems, right? Anticipate the most burning questions people may ask on your social media accounts, and be prepared to respond.

Develop a document that has answers to those questions to make the task of moderating your accounts as easy as possible.

#Strategy

What is the big deal about #Hashtags anyway?

The purposeful use of hashtags is a critical piece to getting your content in front of an entirely new audience.

Essentially, hashtags are content aggregators. You would choose, as a general rule of thumb, three to five key words that have some relevance to your content. The words you choose could also be key words that your target audience would perform a query for that relates to your brand. It is very important that you search hashtags before including them in your posts to ensure that the hashtag does not include any inappropriate content or material that you would not want associated with your brand.

Example: *You are a Wedding Planner in Dallas, Texas posting a picture of a beautiful table you designed at a recent wedding reception. Using hashtags like: #DallasWeddingPlanner #DestinationWeddingPlanner #WeddingDay #LuxuryEventDesigner #BrideToBe are great ways to place your content in front of potential brides searching for a Wedding Planner in Dallas.*

It is also a great idea to create a hashtag that represents your brand that you will include on your posts, almost like a signature. As an example, McDonald's could use a hashtag like #ImLovinIt or perhaps Nike could use #JustDoIt.

These are phrases that are easily associated with these two brands, and would therefore foster brand recognition on social media for them. Do not choose a set of hashtags and make your home with them. There are some, outside of the branded hashtags, that will remain a constant in your posts. However, you should be proactive and ensuring you are using hashtags that are having a positive impact on engagement and follower growth on your accounts. With consistent, strong content, and a good hashtag strategy you will surely begin to see an increase in your followers, engagement, and conversion.

Remember, growing social media is a marathon, not a race.

Short Links

Short links are a great tool to use to track the amount of link clicks within posts on social media, and still maintain a branded look for that content. If you have a long website URL or want to monitor the performance of specific campaign related content (special events, book sales, promotions), URL shorteners help you accomplish this goal. One of the top URL shortener websites is bit.ly. Once logged in to bit.ly, you would copy your desired link and bit.ly generates a shorter link that can also be edited. This way you are able to avoid posting lengthy URL's in social media posts where space and the chance to captivate your audience is limited. Here are a few examples of how short links may look for your organization. Imagine how you can creatively target the use of short links as you develop campaigns and continue to augment your social media strategy.

Example: bit.ly/MySpecialEvent
          bit.ly/BuyMyNewBook

With the continued expansion of domains that are now available, you can now purchase domains and create branded short links for your organization that take the power of this tactic to the next level. To further illustrate, I will use my company as an example. The name of my organization is Mind Your Business, LLC. I acquired a domain that is close to the primary URL I use for my website so I can create links that help me build brand awareness and measure the performance of the links I share online.

Primary website URL: MindYourBizLLC.com

Domain for branded short links: mindbiz.co

Example: mindbiz.co/BuyTheBook
          mindbiz.co/SocialMedia

Mind Your Business!

What pieces of evergreen content can you repurpose across your social media channels?

_____

_____

_____

_____

Brainstorm possible branded hashtags you can use for your organization:

_____

_____

_____

_____

Research and list possible hashtags you can use to attract new followers:

_____

_____

_____

_____

Research possible domains you can use to create branded short links:

_____

_____

_____

_____

So, what is the plan?

"Think ahead. Don't let day-to-day operations drive out planning."
— Donald Rumsfeld

S ocial media can quickly begin to feel like a full-time job if you are approaching it the right way. If you really want to be successful in the digital marketing and social media space, you must plan. Failing to plan is planning to fail.

Developing a social media content calendar will be one of the best ways you can begin to organize your social media plan. You will find it helpful to create a spreadsheet or other type of template to create a visual space to see what is in your social media pipeline. Identify how many times per day and at what times you plan to post. You can write the copy for your posts and include images, links to assets (i.e.: DropBox), links to blog posts etcetera to keep yourself organized. It is okay to post the same content multiple times in a week. In the last chapter, we just explored ways to repurpose content different ways on different platforms. Creating a social media content calendar allows you to manage your social media instead of it managing you.

Manage social media, don't let social media manage you!

You can plan your content days, weeks and even months ahead so you can focus on other aspects of your brand while still building and maintaining a strong presence on social media.

Your social media content calendar should also be used to conduct future audits on your various social media platforms. As you introduce new types of content to your audience, you will need to evaluate its performance to ascertain whether or not you should continue to share that type of content on your accounts.

Once you have planned out your social media strategy on the content calendar, the next step is to schedule it! Manually posting all of the content that needs to be posted on your account would make it very difficult to maintain the consistency needed to see success with your social media.

Social media management and coordination has become a full-time position within large corporations because they recognize the time required to be truly effective in that area. Scheduling content will be huge in the big picture of your Social Media Makeover! People who feel overwhelmed by social media don't have a plan. Even just scheduling your content a week ahead will allow you to stay ahead of the game!

There are several scheduling tools in existence that are user friendly and have other great features that will make this very easy for you. I have my favorites, but my suggestion is to play around with a few options and identify what scheduling tool will best meet the needs of your business. Choose tools that realistically meet your needs and are scalable with the current resources available to your company. Additionally, you want to select a scheduling tool that has analytics already integrated in to the platform. Measuring the success of your content is a very important piece of the pie, and the goal is to keep this simple. A tool with the ability to generate useful reporting will be your best bet.

Delegating The Work

Depending on the resources you have as a business owner and the number of people you have on staff, you may find it advantageous to delegate some aspects of your social media to make operations more effective for your organization. All of the groundwork you have laid in the Social Media Makeover thus far will be useful in helping onboard team members to the task of running your social media like a well-oiled machine without you having to over-see minute details. You can train your team members to learn the voice of your brand. If the person you are bringing on does not have prior experience managing social media, you can train them based on the principles you have learned doing the Social Media Makeover. Many of the cutting-edge social media scheduling tools have features that allow you to add additional users to your account with parameters that allow you to approve the work they schedule, assign them tasks, and communicate within the tool about scheduled content. So, if you are the type that struggles with handing the reigns over to others, there are tools available that allow you to implement a system of checks and balances to create a greater comfort level for you as a manager. In my experience managing social media for different types of organizations, I have observed that it can be a challenging endeavor to attract the right talent to really help you execute your social media strategy. We will delve deeper into the particulars of hiring the right team in a later chapter.

Nevertheless, I definitely recommend completing the Social Media Makeover before making the decision to bring someone on your team. You will have guidelines and a plan in place that defines expectations and draws the blue print of success for them. You want to have an understanding of what successful and effective social media looks for you and your brand, as opposed to depending on another person to define that for you.

Mind Your Business!

Who within your organization will be responsible for developing and managing your content calendar?

_____

_____

_____

_____

In what ways will you prioritize your daily tasks to make time to plan and prepare your social media strategy?

_____

_____

_____

_____

Identify potential obstacles that could hinder planning for social media. Also identify ways to proactively overcome them.

_____

_____

_____

_____

_____

_____

_____

_____

How much is this gonna cost me?

"I think the number one safe haven where people put their money is to invest in yourself first."

– Hill Harper

At its inception, social media was the land of opportunity and perfect place for business owners to get their messages to hundreds, if not thousands of people at once – for FREE! Those days are over, well kind of. Today, on most of the major social media platforms, algorithms have been implemented that have a significant impact on who sees your content. In general, to maximize who sees what you post, you need to boost your content, or pay a certain amount of money increase the exposure of your content. It is still very possible to reach people organically, meaning without boosting your content, but it takes a great amount of engagement (likes, shares, comments) from your following to accomplish that.

The bottom line is, as a business owner, you will need to make a small investment in your social media content to reach your intended target audience. No matter what product or services you offer, you have to make an investment in yourself; That includes marketing and how you get your message out to the world. You don't have to have a huge budget to achieve this – do what is realistic for you (Think S.M.A.R.T.) One of the benefits of investing in paid ad spends is it allows you to target who you want to reach using a very specific criteria of attributes, thereby allowing you to cater to those most interested in your content. Being able to define the desired audience of your posts allows you to put your posts in front of who you outlined in the target persona you completed earlier, and maximize return on your investment.

According to Hootsuite, "Analysts predicted a 26.3 percent global increase on spending for social media ads." The Nielsen Company asserts "Social media is one of the biggest opportunities that companies across industries have to connect directly to consumers." You do not have to have big money to be an effective business that leverages the power of social media to reach potential clients – just be strategic.

Let's explore the trifecta of media types within the social media space:

Owned Media – {website, blog, social media} Owned media refers to the various elements of your digital footprint that all work together to expand the reach of your brand online. Your website, blog, email campaigns, and social media all comprise this category. The more real estate you have in owned media, the greater opportunity you have to develop brand equity and improve your search engine ranking.

Earned Media – {shares, reposts, mentions, testimonials} Earned media is the activity that happens through actions such as: likes, shares, reposts, and mentions. This is the type of media that makes being effective with your content and SEO strategies very important. In short, it is the online version of the word on the street. Is your message worth spreading?

Paid Media – {social media ads, retargeting, search/display ads, pay-per-click ads} Paid media is the content you invest in that has the objective to drive people to your owned media properties and increase earned media. You can set up campaign's online that drive traffic and increase conversions to your website from your social media channels. With the increase in complexity of social media algorithms, the need for paid media campaigns is definitely on the rise. Allocate funds in your marketing budget so that you maintain a competitive edge in the digital marketplace.

This trifecta of media types is important to understand as you decide how and where to allocate budget dollars within your social media strategy. All of these elements work in tandem to your brand's benefit when leveraged through strategic use of SEO and Content Marketing.

When you make the investment in paid ad spends, make the time investment to analyze how the content performed and use that data to make adjustments that will improve the performance of future ads. Remember, now that you are undergoing the Social Media Makeover, your strategies are data-driven.

Mind Your Business!

How have you used paid ads for your business?

_____

_____

_____

_____

What did you learn from the experience? What did the data tell you about your audience?

_____

_____

_____

_____

What types of content do you share that would benefit from being a part of a paid media spend?

_____

_____

_____

_____

Making Dollars Make Sense

"I am big advocate of financial intelligence."
– Daymond John

Be a savvy entrepreneur and begin to identify ways to monetize your social media. You have to get a return on your time investment you have made building an awesome social media strategy. There should always be a "why" behind everything you post on social media. You should have a call to action for anything you share on a social network. All of your content should be a part of a greater plan to steer your target audience in the direction of a desired action or response- Which should be a fiduciary relationship if you are a business owner. For example, let's say you are an author trying to promote awareness of your latest literary work. You would include a call to action like "Visit MyWebsite.com now to purchase your copy of "My Awesome Book"! in every post. Never under estimate the power of the ask! You have to call your audience to some sort of action with every post. Direct them to visit your website for more information! Tell them where to go in order to purchase your product! Encourage them to register for an event you are hosting! This should be the first step in your sales funnel to convert your social media activity into clients!

Treat your social media as a repository for opportunities to generate passive income. It is a platform that you have access to in order to sell yourself and your products, use it wisely! It should not be the only way you are generating interest in, or creating exposure for your business. The mere fact this content can be scheduled means you have a platform to get the word out about your business to a large audience, while you are doing other things to grow your business – capitalize on this!

Monetizing your social media is going to be a very individual thing as it depends on what your goals and objectives are, the industry you are in, and the behaviors of your target audience – but it should be a part of your plan nevertheless.

Mind Your Business!

What are your primary calls to action for your products or services?

_____

_____

_____

_____

What opportunities do you see to monetize activity on social media?

_____

_____

_____

_____

Are you currently generating leads from your social media?

_____

_____

_____

_____

Social media is great, but…

"Do not go where the path may lead, go instead where there is no path and leave a trail."

– Ralph Waldo Emerson

Is one of your goals for your social media to increase the amount of followers you have? That is a great goal to have as it will expose your brand to more people and hopefully translate into more business for your company. Can I ask you a question? What would you do if one day, your social media accounts were mysteriously shut down? Or what about if one day, Mark Zuckerberg, CEO of Facebook, decided to close the doors of the company and delete everybody's accounts. How would you reach the followers you worked so hard to gain?

You have to create a way outside of your social media accounts to access your target audience. Beyond social media, you have to build your list, or database of clients and find a way to unobtrusively touch them on a regular business. One of the tactics you use on your social media should be a call to action that leads to prospective clients providing you with at least an email address you can use to add them to a customer relationship management or email marketing solution. There are a few great options of email tools that allow you to create templates you can use to share some of the same information you are sharing on social media. The objective here is to not rely on social media as the only touch point you have with clients and potential clients. Depending on the following you have amassed on social media, it could be devastating to your sales funnel to lose access to that audience – be proactive about having a greater control of client information!

Here a few suggestions you can implement into your social media strategy that will help you grow your list outside of your social media platforms – remember, this isn't about followers, it is about collecting customer/client information.

- Blog – Always encourage readers to enter their email to get notified of new blogs or to receive other exclusive content. Seek opportunities to be featured on other blogs related to your industry. This will send interested parties to your blog/website looking to learn more about what you offer.
- Do a giveaway – Give away one of your products, but require an email address to enter the contest.
- Ensure your website is optimized for opt-ins – There should be a place on your website where visitors can sign-up for a newsletter or to receive other content.
- Exclusive Offers or Content – Create exclusivity around being on your email list! If the concept resonates with your target audience, they will take the bait!
- Put it in the bag – If you have a tangible product, when you fulfill orders include collateral encouraging them to sign-up to receive special offers or exclusive content.
- Host an event – It could be a launch party, book signing, or a mixer; Whatever the event is, collect those emails in order to register. Be sure to have a way to collect them onsite in case someone slipped through the cracks or came as a guest.

Mind Your Business!

What are you doing to build your email list?

_____

_____

_____

_____

What type of content or incentives are you offering to encourage people to join your email list?

_____

_____

_____

_____

What types of posts can you share on social media that will lead followers to your website?

_____

_____

_____

_____

Managing Your Social Media Team

"Talent wins games, but teamwork and intelligence win championships"

- Michael Jordan

After completing the first edition of *The Social Media Makeover*, I realized that something more is needed for the readers who manage social media as a business unit within an organization.

Managing a team of social media professionals is a unique undertaking. The implementation of systems, organization and clear communication will be a huge part of your team's success.

Your first order of business needs to be the development of standard operating procedures.

Standard Operating Procedures

Standard operating procedures are an essential part of a high-functioning and productive team. Standard operating procedures make expectations clear, foster accountability and make tasks replicable by anyone who might assume these responsibilities at a later time. As you work to develop standard operating procedures, consider every task that is executed by members of your team. Involve the experts within your team to write your standard operating procedures as you want to ensure these are developed thoroughly and with consideration of all possible outcomes. Here are some basic bullet points that should be included in your standard operating procedures:

Organizational Chart - The reporting structure of your teams should be made crystal clear to everyone. This document should be maintained and updated when personnel changes occur within the organization.

Detailed explanations of tasks - Every possible process, within teams and cross-functionally should be outlined with clarity and detail. This should cover functional operational tasks as well requests from other departments. Not only does this keep staff accountable for what is required of them, but it acts as a training tool for new additions to teams and gives volunteers an idea of expectations as well. You can develop your own templates to best fit the needs of your brand, but making sure the below are at the core of your procedures should ensure you have comprehensive procedures documented.

Refer to these key elements as a rubric to ensure you are drafting a clear and cogent document.

1. Policy – What organizational standard does this policy need to meet?
2. Purpose – What is the rationale or reason for this procedure?
3. Scope – What areas of your organization are affected by this procedure?
4. Responsibilities – Who is listed in this procedure, and what do they need to do?
5. Definitions – What jargon will be mentioned in this procedure that the layperson will not be familiar with?
6. Procedures and Methodologies – What are the specific steps or tasks for this procedure? Be specific.
7. Effectiveness Criteria – What is the measurement for success or completion for this procedure?

Mind Your Business!

Do you currently have standard operating procedures in place?

_____

_____

_____

_____

What systems and processes do you have in place to help your team operate efficiently?

_____

_____

_____

_____

Who will be responsible for drafting your standard operating procedures?

_____

_____

_____

_____

Hiring the right talent

"The dictionary is the only place that success comes before work."
- Vince Lombardi, Jr.

As you work to build your social media team, there are certain traits that you will need to look for in your prospects. It is very important that you do your due diligence in your search for a rock star Social Media Manager. The time and effort that it will require for you to properly onboard them to your organization and acclimate them to the voice of your brand would be wasted on an employee brought on through a hasty rushed hiring decision.

Identifying a potential candidate with the right mix of technical savvy and soft skills will ultimately be the winning combination for you and your organization. It can be a challenging endeavor to attract the right talent to help you execute your social media strategy. Here are ten things to look for {skill sets and traits} of potential candidates you may be considering hiring to manage your social media:

Strong writing skills – Content is king in the world of social media. The credibility of your brand is compromised when you have poor grammar and less than captivating content on your social media platforms. It is necessary that anyone managing your social media accounts have strong writing skills.

Ingenuity – The only constant in the digital marketing and social media space is change. You need someone who is creative and able to continually bring fresh ideas to the table to help you remain competitive amongst your industry peers.

Tech Savvy– This one may seem like a no-brainer, but trust me when I say it isn't. You may be surprised to learn that there are many people who only ever use social media platforms from mobile devices. Social media platforms offer businesses more robust features that are only accessible on desktops and are vital for a social media manager to use in order to be successful. Make sure that the person is comfortable not only "navigating" the social media networks, but that they have the aptitude to use things like social media scheduling tools and spreadsheets.

Flexible – This probably should have been the first skill set I mentioned. Flexibility is very important. You need someone who realizes that no matter the industry you are in, with the best plans in place, the unexpected is inevitable. A strong candidate will be willing and able to adapt to hitting the curve balls and catching the pop fly's that sometimes come along with managing social media well. Getting that understanding up front will alleviate great misunderstanding later.

Proactive – You need a person that will keep a very close eye on emerging trends in the digital space. Things change in the realm of social media often, and you need someone to keep your brand at the forefront of those changes. You also need a person who will be proactive about making suggestions of strategic ways to implement emerging trends and new options for content on your account.

Analytical Skills – You have conducted an audit on your social media platforms, so you have gotten a taste of the many different sets of metrics that are available to assess how content is performing on your accounts. You need someone that is comfortable running those reports and interpreting the data so they can make the requisite changes and recommendations as needed.

Creative – Graphic design and video production are essential parts of high-performing content on social media. A good candidate does not necessarily need to be a graphic designer or have video editing skills, but what is crucial is the skill to be able to effectively communicate ideas for creative concepts to graphic designers and video editors. If they have the prowess to be able to get designers to interpret their creative vision for concepts, they are still winning in this area. Your social media team needs to also be able to continuously ideate, innovate and create on behalf of your brand.

A people person – It is important that your Social Media Manager responds to users on your social media platforms. This could be anything from acknowledging favorable comments from users to handling complaints. The person managing your account needs to have the ability to interact in a manner that is client focused and service driven. This will increase engagement on your accounts, which works towards your bottom line.

Project Manager – The candidate does not need any particular certifications in this area, just the ability to create campaigns for various initiatives on your social media accounts and develop a tactical plan to ensure it happens. The prioritization of tasks, multi-tasking, and organizational skills needed to be a rock star Social Media Manager can't be emphasized enough.

Team Player – If you are going to delegate the management of your social media to another person, you need them to be a team player; The kind that is collaborative and relatable. They need to not only be able to manage the work but the relationships with those around them they may need to rely on to get the job done.

This list is not all-inclusive, but it will definitely give you a good start. I would recommend that you give strong consideration to other skills, talents, and attributes that may more closely align with the specific structure and culture of your organization and add them to this list.

Now that you have identified some of the skills that will be required for a successful Social Media Manager, let's look at how you can get them in the door!

Job Descriptions

A solid job description will be one of your first lines of defense in attracting the right talent to your organization. You may or may not have the support of a Human Resources department to assist you in the development of an appropriate job description, so I have provided samples for you to adapt to your organization. This is your first opportunity to set the tone and expectation for what their role will be in your organization. You want to paint an accurate picture of what will be required for the candidate to be successful in this role, but you do not want to give them the keys to the kingdom. Unfortunately, many people feel because they engage on social media personally, they have the requisite skills to do it in a professional environment. With that being said, save some things for the interview. You want to avoid unintentionally feeding the candidate the formula to get through your hiring process.

You will see a job description for a Social Media Coordinator and a Social Media Manager. The key skill differentiator between the two descriptions is the Social Media Manager can be typically found to have additional responsibilities, more approval authority and administrative access than their coordinator counterpart.

In some instances, the Social Media Coordinator may report to the Social Media Manager. Feel free to make adjustments to meet your individual needs as a hiring manager.

Job Title: Social Media Coordinator
{Include a description of your organization here. This sets the tone and is the applicant's first touch point of the culture of the company}

Job Description:
We are seeking an innovative and talented Social Media Coordinator to help us maintain a dynamic social media presence for our organization. The Social Media Coordinator will be responsible for managing the day-to-day social media strategy while proactively seeking to identify ways to enhance that strategy.

Essential Duties:
- Curate, schedule and manage all published content for use across Social media platforms that support corporate goals and objectives.
- Monitor, listen and engage with end-users to foster a sense of community online and brand loyalty.
- Create and oversee marketing campaigns and targeted promotions of varying scope and complexity.
- Deliver regular reports that analyze content performance across social media platforms with the ability to convey and interpret complex data to other business units.
- Maintain a working knowledge of social media trends, applications and best practices.
- Work collaboratively with Graphic Designer/Video Production/Key Stakeholders to maintain brand consistency and harmonization.

Qualifications & Experience:
- Excellent written and oral communication skills.
- Motivated self-starter with strong organization skills
- Experience with the widely adapted social media platforms
- Bachelor's degree in Marketing, PR, Communications or equivalent work experience

Job Title: Social Media Manager
Include a description of your organization here. This sets the tone and is
the applicant's first touch point of the culture of the company}

Job Description:
We are seeking a focused, driven, and goal-oriented Social Media Manager
to provide leadership and creative direction to our Social Media
Coordinators. The Social Media Manager will ensure that a cohesive, and
competitive social media strategy is maintained across social media
platforms.

Essential Duties:
- Train and develop Social Media Coordinators. Facilitates content
  ideation and reinforces best practices that support the overall
  company social media strategy.
- Maintain a working knowledge of current social media trends,
  applications, and best practices and identify ways to implement
  them into the current strategy.
- Develop and strengthen relationships across business units to
  cultivate a collaborative work-environment and ensure brand
  consistency.
- Regularly analyze reporting data to ensure content is resonating
  with the target audience. Guide and direct the Social Media
  Coordinator toward best practices.

Experience Required:
- 2-3 years work experience as a Social Media Coordinator
- Strong leadership and interpersonal skills; Advanced problem-
  solving skills
- Content creation and copywriting skills; Expert knowledge of SEO
  and Analytics.
- Excellent written and oral communication skills; the ability to
  deliver messages with tact and diplomacy.
- Expert, proven knowledge of social media and digital marketing
  strategies and tactics.
- Bachelor's degree in Marketing, PR, Communications or equivalent
  work experience

Let's Talk!

So, you have put out a solid description of what your needs are for your organization's social media; the next step is the interview process. As I mentioned earlier, it is highly likely that you will encounter candidates who feel qualified for the job because they use social media personally. The interview is where you can separate the casual users from those who will be invaluable assets to your team. It pains me to say this, but the interview for a role like is very easy to fake your way through – I have personally been hoodwinked by a person I thought was a strong candidate. Once this individual joined the team, it did not take long at all to see they were not equipped for the job. This scenario brings to mind the adage, "Be slow to hire and quick to fire."

That experience led me to look at the interview process for members of the social media team a bit differently. You still want to ask them the standard and customary questions to assess their experience and familiarity with certain areas, but I also strongly encourage you to ask a series of situational questions and interactive scenarios to get a good idea of the strength of the candidate. Again, this is designed to be a blueprint for you. Please make any changes necessary to make this fit your organization.

Sample Interview Questions

- As a Social Media Coordinator/Manager, how would you keep yourself organized?
- What is your leadership and/or communication style within a team environment?
- Tell me about your experience using analytics to augment your social media strategy.
- What would your process be for learning the voice of our brand?
- What is SEO and what role do you feel it plays in social media?
- How is ROI defined in the realm of social media?
- Do you feel it is important to schedule content in advance?
- What scheduling tools have you used?
- How would you respond to a troll account or an individual posting negative comments about our company?
- How do you stay on top of new trends and features?
- In what scenarios would you choose to use paid media campaigns for this organization?
- Discuss a few of the best practices and suggested actions to avoid on Facebook, Twitter, Instagram, and YouTube.

Sample Interview Scenarios:

- Ask the candidate to write sample copy for posts that could be shared on any of your social media platforms. This will show how they respond in unplanned situations and give you an unfiltered sample of their writing abilities.
- Ask the candidate to share with you any areas of opportunity they identified as they looked at your social media accounts. Clearly, they exist, or they would not be needed on the team. This will show you if this person has any creative value to offer as you continue to augment your social media strategy.
- Generate a recent report showing the analytics of the activity on your social media accounts. Ask the candidate to interpret the report and ask them what suggestions they would make based on the data.
- If the candidate will be working in a fast-paced environment that requires them to cover live events, simulate that environment for them and ask them to "cover the event." This is a great way to see how they perform under pressure.
- Ask the candidate to discuss a sample campaign they would initiate to increase engagement and followers on _your_ social media accounts. This exercise will highlight whether or not they have researched your organization in preparation for the interview and if they have ideas that complement your strategy and tactical plan.
- Give the candidate an example of a potential public relations/online reputation crisis. Ask them to outline their plan to manage and diffuse the situation.

Mind Your Business!

What are your processes for attracting talent?

_____

_____

_____

_____

What characteristics and traits can you add that will help you make a good hiring choice?

_____

_____

_____

_____

What can you add to the sample interview questions that will help you make a good hiring choice?

_____

_____

_____

_____

Managing Daily Operations

"Most of what we call management consists of making it difficult for people to get their work done."

- Peter Drucker

The management of the daily operations of your social media team needs to be consistent. Without consistency, established guidelines, and clear expectations there is bound to be a disorder.

There are essential functions within your social media team that should have clearly defined standard operating procedures as they are the core of efficiency for your team.

Maintaining order and efficient systems are what make social media manageable. Without implementing a strong systematic plan, social media can be a very stressful undertaking, which is exactly what you want to avoid.

This is one of the strongest tools in your arsenal that you have to position your team to win on social media.

Let's explore The Social Media Workflow.

The Social Media Workflow

Social Media
Audit

Editorial
Needs
Assessment

Asset Design
& Production
Requests

Editorial
Calendar

Schedule
Content

Weekly
Reporting

Social Media Audit

We covered the social media audit in greater detail in the first chapter, however, I cannot stress enough the importance of conducting audits on your social media platforms regularly. Your team will need to take a frequent, (I suggest weekly) assessment of how content is performing on your social media accounts. Each social media platform has its own set of metrics that can be measured to determine whether or not content you are posting is performing well. You will have to determine what metrics are most important to measure success for your organization. You will need to run these reports so you can make adjustments to content if it is not resonating with your intended target audience.

Editorial Needs Assessment

What do you have coming up on your organization's master calendar? Are there any promotions coming up soon? Is there an event you are hosting that you need to begin advertisement for? Beyond things that are scheduled on the master calendar, there may be blog content or other types of operational and evergreen content that you rotate into the schedule. Identifying what is coming up, and adding standard regularly scheduled content will help you find the gaps in your content calendar so you can ensure you are maintaining consistency in the posting frequency across all platforms.

Asset Design & Production Requests

Depending on your organizations' staffing capacity, you may have dedicated resources that are responsible for the design or production of graphics and video assets that will be utilized on your social media platforms. How much lead time do these teams require to create these assets? Are there other requirements they have when requests are submitted? After you have established what these guidelines are, they should be documented in a standard operating procedure, and strictly adhered to in an effort to ensure this process is smooth and friction does not occur between these teams.

Editorial/Content Calendar

There should be a shared access document that contains the intended schedule for social media content. Shared access to the editorial or content calendar gives key stakeholders and management the opportunity to review and approve proposed content as a form of checks and balances to ensure the planned content moves the established social media strategy forward. Depending on the needs and culture of your organization, this has the potential to be a very fluid document. Define a point at which content is finalized so that it can be scheduled.

Schedule Content

Once the editorial/content calendar has been approved, it can be scheduled in the designated tool for posting across your social media platforms. Establish the timeline and expectation for the scheduling of content so that your team stays accountable to completing this task. Scheduling content frees them up to complete other necessary tasks and ensures consistency in recommended posting times across platforms. Since consistency is such an important factor in a successful social media strategy, you want to manage adherence to this area closely, so your strategy does not lose momentum.

Weekly Reporting

You have to establish which Key Performance Indicators (KPI's) are important for your organization. Once you have determined what data is needed to assess the effectiveness of your social media strategy, weekly reports need to be compiled and delivered to examine how content performed that week. This report goes hand-in-hand with the social media audit. Additionally, if you have a targeted promotion or marketing campaign running, you may also need to capture segmented data specific to the related content to measure its performance outside of your "regularly scheduled programming."

Moreover, key stakeholders may have individual interests in the performance of certain for various reasons. Establish a process for the request of this data because time is of the essence to ensure the accuracy of the information provided. As long as the content is alive on a platform, KPI's like reach, engagement, video views and amplification rate will continue to tabulate. What does this mean? Although you may run a query for a specific date range for content, it may not be a true reflection of the activity that occurred during that range of time. Communication about what your organization's reporting needs are will help keep the numbers clean and the strategy decisions sound.

Mind Your Business!

How will you apply The Social Media Workflow to your team? Who will you delegate tasks to?

_____

_____

_____

_____

_____

_____

_____

_____

_____

_____

_____

_____

_____

_____

_____

_____

_____

_____

_____

Effective Leadership

"My idea of management is that what your job is as the boss is to find really good people and empower them and leave them alone."
- Ruth Reichl

Completing a Social Media Makeover, and then subsequently failing to successfully manage those who handle the day to day operations for you, essentially negates the hard work that was poured into changing the trajectory of your social media strategy. Sure you want to attract an amazingly qualified individual to join your organization; but do you have what it takes to retain them? It has been said that people do not quit jobs, they quit bosses. Striking the right balance between managing an operation that meets and exceeds performance objectives, but still cultivates an environment that fosters creativity and inspires your team to chase success is crucial. Does this describe your leadership style? The following pages will give you some helpful suggestions you can implement to lead a team of champion social media and digital marketing professionals.

To begin, here are some suggested actions, tactics and just general things to consider that will help you win as a leader, and things a good leader should avoid.

Let's get into it!

Ways to Win as a Leader

- Keep the lines of communication open and clear. People want to feel like their input and expertise is needed, valued and appreciated. Make your door a safe threshold to cross to share those thoughts and ideas.
- Hold regular meetings to discuss what pending projects and deliverables are in the pipeline and the role they play in those areas. Keeping your team informed and engaged in the big picture will keep synergy and collaborative energy among them.
- Reward your team for hard work and stellar performance. Let's face it; most people are not intrinsically motivated. Simple acts of recognition and reward will incentivize them to keep exceeding expectations. It is a win-win situation, just do it.
- Stay aligned with the other business units you and your team rely upon to get the job done. Proactively seeking to gain an understanding of what other contributors need will build trust and will ultimately move your social media strategy forward.
- Get creative input from key stakeholders when developing marketing campaigns for them. Sure, this space may be outside of their area of expertise, ask them anyway! Getting their input and buy-in to the plan will inadvertently turn them into a Brand Ambassador, which benefits you in the end. Play nice in the sandbox.
- Make sure your team has the necessary credentials and access to the tools and resources needed to get their work done efficiently. It is to your benefit that your team is under the impression that you are their advocate for success.

- Get to know your team. Beyond their requisite skill sets and experience that got them in the door, what is their personality type? Making an effort to understand this side of your team will help you manage and delegate tasks better. How can you accomplish this? Plan team building activities and observe the dynamics. Personality tests like DISC or Myers-Briggs can provide useful information about the attitudes and behaviors of individuals. Turn taking the personality test into an exercise in getting to know one another better to work better together as a team – who wouldn't be open to that? It serves that purpose and gives you valuable information as their manager.
- Create and/or provide opportunities for training and development. Investing in the growth of your team's knowledge and skillsets is a mutually beneficial ROI. They will take greater ownership of the role they play in the organization, and you reap the benefits of enhanced performance as a result of newly acquired skills.

Things a good Leader should avoid

- Don't refuse to delegate work. You cannot be everywhere all of the time. Implement a functional plan that keeps your operation running smoothly in your absence. Steer clear of creating an environment in which decisions and processes come to a standstill if you are not there to put down your stamp of approval.
- Don't discredit or undervalue the creative input of your team. You made a thorough and carefully considered hiring decision when you brought them onboard, allow them to bring their breadth of knowledge and experience to the table.
- Don't make things up as you go. It can be very frustrating to never have an understanding of what is expected and/or required of you. Making arbitrary changes to policies and processes is a breeding ground for contention and breaks in productivity. Rely on the standard operating procedure documents you developed, and make revisions as needed.
- Don't make assumptions. Filling in gaps in communication with assumptions is an indication of a lack of emotional intelligence on your part as a manager. Communication will in almost every case, make things clear. Get the buy-in from key stakeholders about the creative and strategic direction for their campaigns (It will keep you from having to re-do work later). Additionally, give your team members the benefit of the doubt in every situation you can.
- Don't be opposed to exploring and implementing new trends in social media and digital marketing – even if only on a trial basis. Doing things "as you have always done them" is not a winning strategy in this ever-changing environment. Don't negate your Social Media Makeover.

- Don't be inconsistent in holding team members accountable for deficits in performance and dependability. Everyone's contribution to the Social Media Workflow is needed. Run a tight, but a fair ship.
- Don't overwork your team. If your social media accounts are demanding or is an influencer/celebrity account, distribute the workload in such a way that allows them to be effective and creative in one or two areas as opposed to being mediocre in several.
- Don't be reactive, be proactive! Some things are simply NOT a surprise in your organization – Be prepared! It will increase efficiencies and decrease bottlenecks in the workflow because of "last-minute requests" that you knew were coming your way.

Emotional Intelligence

Daniel Goleman, the Psychologist who helped to popularize Emotional Intelligence asserts there are five key elements to it. An emotionally intelligent leader is going to be a very successful leader in any organization. The rigors of what being effective and productive in the digital marketing industry mandate make it necessary for an effective leader to have these qualities and characteristics. Your emotions and responses to things impact your team. You drive the culture of the team, so why foster an environment of collective emotional intelligence?

Let's get into it!

The Five Elements of Emotional Intelligence

1. **Self-Awareness** – Self-awareness typically means you have a strong grasp on where your strengths and weaknesses exist, and that you are humble enough to make improvements where needed. Remain cognizant of how you are leading your team, and the ways in which you respond to tough situations.

2. **Self-Regulation** – Self-regulators maintain a cool head during the hottest moments. If you are managing enterprise digital marketing and social media, then you have undoubtedly encountered hot moments. Be intentional, calm and calculated about how to respond to your team, cross-functional departments and other stakeholders.

3. **Motivation** – You are likely charged with leading your team because you are a self-driven go-getter. Even high-achievers need motivation from time to time. It is not going to always come from the outsiders, but remain optimistic.

Don't negate the importance of self-care to help you recharge your batteries from time to time.

4. **Empathy** – This is a mission critical characteristic to have as a leader as it is a main ingredient for building trust, loyalty and respect amongst your team. You can't be all business, all of the time. Be in tune with the needs of your team that go beyond the work they are responsible for.

5. **Social Skills** – Hopefully, being a social butterfly is an easy task for a person leading a team of social media pros! Social skills are going to be very helpful when it comes to celebrating wins (big and small) with your team and for conflict management. Be purposeful about creating "fun" moments to decompress with those you lead.

Mind Your Business!

How would describe your leadership style?

_____

_____

_____

_____

What are your opportunities for improvement as a leader?

_____

_____

_____

_____

How will you develop the areas you feel are opportunities?

_____

_____

_____

_____

Suggested Tools and Applications

A s you take on the journey to implementing the Social Media Makeover in your organization, you are going to need a solid set of resources to get started. Here a few tools and applications I suggest that will be useful, particularly those of you that you do not have graphic designers and video editors available to you. These tools are easy to use, have small learning curves, and are reasonably priced. I have also included these suggestions because of their longevity and continued adaptation to new developments in the social media realm. Some are free and others require a modestly priced subscription, but they will prove to be very helpful as you work on your Social Media Makeover.

Social Media Scheduling Tools

⇒ Hootsuite
⇒ CoSchedule
⇒ Sprout Social

Graphics Creation Tools/Apps

⇒ Canva
⇒ WordSwag
⇒ Ripl

Analytics & Reporting Tools

⇒ The native platform (Facebook, Instagram, Twitter, etc.)
⇒ Google Analytics
⇒ Sprout Social

Video Editing

⇒ Vegas Movie Studio
⇒ Wondershare Filmora

Asset Repository and File Sharing

⇒ Dropbox
⇒ Google Drive

Photo Editing

⇒ Lightroom CC
⇒ Snapseed

Credential Management

⇒ LastPass

URL Shorteners

⇒ bit.ly – bitly.com
⇒ goo.gl – Type this into your browser
⇒ owl.ly – Powered by Hootsuite
⇒ GoDaddy
⇒ Network Solutions

Royalty-Free Music Sources for Videos

⇒ FreeMusicArchive.org
⇒ MusOpen.org
⇒ YouTube.com/audiolibrary/soundeffects

Mind Your Business!

Take an inventory of the tools you are using for social media. Do you need to make any updates?

_____

_____

_____

_____

_____

_____

_____

_____

How can you streamline the tools you are currently using to improve the efficiency of your social media strategy?

_____

_____

_____

_____

_____

_____

_____

_____

Power Tips

Facebook

- **Business is Business** – Don't use a personal page for your brand. Set up a business page and create a Business Manager account to easily manage your paid media activity.

- **Establish a Budget** – Put a little cash behind your most important content to give it a boost. Exclusively sharing organic content will not give you the lift your business needs to grow.

- **Post natively** – Even though you should now have an amazing scheduling tool, on occasion, upload video natively for a greater reach.

- **Be social** – Be sure and tag others as appropriate to increase the reach of your posts. Engage with users by responding promptly to comments and direct messages.

- **Do you like me?** – Be sure you have the Facebook widget embedded on your website and in your email signature so people can easily link to your page.

- **Stay in the loop** – Facebook is constantly making changes to the platform to improve the user experience. Keep your ear to the ground so you always on the cutting-edge of available features.

Instagram

- **Only the best will do** – ALWAYS use high quality images and video. Period.
- **Hashtag** – These content aggregators are integral to getting your content in front of new eyes – but don't overdo it. You can only use 30 hashtags per post. If you are going to use more than 5-7 hashtags in a post, post them in a comment instead. It will keep you're the look of your copy cleaner.
- **Contact information in bio** – Make sure the link in your profile works and all of the contact information is current.
- **Establish a budget** – Facebook and Instagram are linked, so your strategy to boost certain content will go hand in hand with your efforts on Facebook – be strategic.
- **Follow me!** – Be sure you have the Instagram widget embedded on your website and in your email signature so people can easily link to your page.
- **Shake things up!** – Add variety to your timeline. Post video and static images alternatively. Use the feature that allows you to post several images and/or video in one post to maximize how you share moments

Twitter

- **Keep it short** – You have a limited number of characters available to get your point across, make them count!
- **Pin it!** – Pin an important tweet or introductory video to the top of your timeline, make a great impression.
- **Talk to strangers** – Twitter is an easy place to engage with others in your industry, don't be afraid to network with influencers in your industry.
- **Action!** – Video performs exceptionally well on Twitter, use that to your advantage.
- **Schedule it** – Take advantage of the Media Studio within Twitter to schedule video content that may be larger than what your scheduling tool has the capacity to handle.
- **Establish a Budget** – Put a little cash behind your most important content to give it more exposure.
- **Increase your likes** – Be sure you have the Twitter widget embedded on your website and in your email signature so people can easily link to your page.

YouTube

- **Make it searchable** – YouTube is highest used search engine after Google. Link your Google+ account to maximize SEO.

- **Key Words are the key** – Make sure you have completed the channel key words with the words relevant to your content, this how your videos will appear in the area for suggested viewing.

- **Follow the rules** – Do not share copyrighted content on your page as it could lead to your page being disabled.

- **Become a pro** – There are several tools out there to jazz up the quality of your video content. The competition is stiff is most industries, so make sure you stand out among the crowd.

- **Encourage them to tune in** – Be sure you have the YouTube widget embedded on your website and in your email signature so people can easily link to your page.

- **Make them feel welcomed** – Take the time to customize your cover art, and record a trailer for your page that visitors will see when they first visit your page. It creates a more polished look and makes you look like the professional you are!

Mind Your Business!

How can you combine the unique selling proposition of your brand with the power tips to strengthen your efforts on social media?

_____

_____

_____

_____

_____

_____

_____

_____

_____

_____

_____

_____

_____

_____

_____

_____

_____

_____

_____

_____

_____

_____

_____

_____

_____

A few final thoughts…

It is my hope that The Social Media Makeover has helped to guide your tactical and strategic plan for the social media in your organization, and how you approach leading your team. Social media can indeed be quite the undertaking, but with a well-executed plan, success is always within your reach.

The most challenging part of the Social Media Makeover is "Discovering Your Why". It can be very tough to really hone in on who you are trying to reach. It can be so easy to fall in to the trap of "keeping up with the Joneses" in your industry and posting things with no strategy behind it – Don't do it! You have to remain focused on reaching the client that is uniquely drawn to what you are offering. Once you have clearly defined that audience, the rest is easy! At that point, developing content and planning it out then becomes like inviting a close friend over for a meal. You know them like the back of your hand. You know everything they like. So with that knowledge, preparing a meal for them isn't a laborious chore because it makes you happy to prepare something special you know they will enjoy.

Your social media strategy is going to be an ever-evolving thing. Social media itself changes, new platforms are born, and your objectives as a business owner shift. Just be flexible and adaptive – keep up with it, the payoff is worthwhile for your brand. I hope you refer to The Social Media Makeover often. Don't be intimidated by the audit! Refer to the skills and traits that a successful Social Media Manager should have! Remember there is power in the ask! The very fact that you have read this book, says you care about the success of your business. Implement what has been shared, and see for yourself that the sky is the limit.

"Go confidently in the direction of your dreams. Live the life you have imagined." – Henry David Thoreau

About The Author

Tisha Holman is a digital marketing, brand and social media Strategist that has helped organizations large and small implement strategies to elevate their digital presence. She is an industry expert dedicated to sharing knowledge that helps organizations from all industries solidify the foundation their businesses are built upon, and win in the digital marketing vertical. Tisha is the CEO and Founder of Mind Your Business, LLC, and has been featured on ABC, CBS, FOX and The CW, as well spoken on stages domestic and international sharing her insights and expertise. In her spare time, Tisha enjoys great food, travel, giving back to her community and spending time with her beautiful and talented daughter, Sydney Alexandria, the one who inspires her to reach for the stars.

Tisha is also the Author of *Lights! Camera! Action!: Get Your Brand On Television* and *Go Ye Into All The World Wide Web.*

www.MindYourBizLLC.com

www.ingramcontent.com/pod-product-compliance
Lightning Source LLC
LaVergne TN
LVHW051709050326
832903LV00032B/4092